DEC **THIS BOOK BELONGS TO** 93

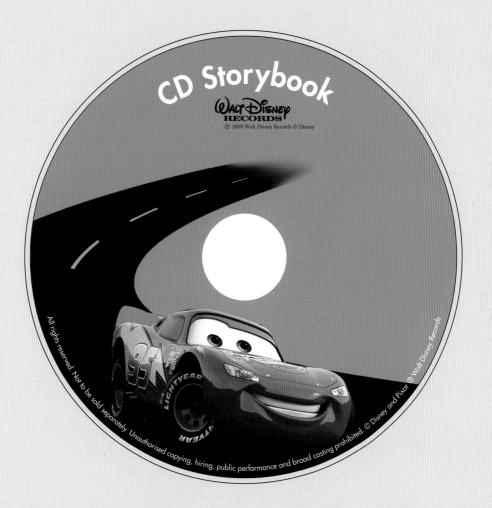

CD Storybook

Walt Disney
RECORDS
℗ 2008 Walt Disney Records © Disney

Characters (in order of appearance)
Narrator   David Jeremiah
Not Chuck   Mike "No Name" Nelson
Lightning McQueen   Owen Wilson
Mack   John Ratzenberger
Sheriff   Michael Wallis
Mater   Larry the Cable Guy
Doc Hudson   Paul Newman
Sally   Bonnie Hunt
Luigi   Tony Shalhoub
Flo   Jenifer Lewis
Kori Turbowitz   Sarah Clark
Additional Voices   Kathy Coates
Bob Cutlass   Bob Costas
The King   Richard Petty

Read-along Story Produced by Randy Thornton
and Ted Kryczko
Co-produced and Engineered by Jeff Sheridan
Adapted by David Watts
Creative Direction by Steve Gerdes
Design by David Braucher
℗ Walt Disney Records/Pixar
© Disney/Pixar. All rights reserved.

This edition published by Parragon in 2008
Parragon Books Ltd
Queen Street House
4 Queen Street
Bath, BA1 1HE, UK

ISBN 978-1-4054-7259-3
Manufactured in China

Bath New York Singapore Hong Kong Cologne Delhi Melbourne

It was the final race of the season and Lightning McQueen was in the lead. It looked like he was about to become the first rookie to ever win the Piston Cup. There was just one problem – he wouldn't listen to his pit crew. "We need tyres now, come on!"

McQueen yelled, "No, no, no, no – no tyres, just gas!" Then he roared back onto the track. "Chequered flag, here I come."

But he should have listened because on the final turn his rear tyres blew out. As McQueen desperately lunged for the finish line, his two top competitors, The King and Chick Hicks, caught up with him. It was a photo finish and a three-way tie!

It was decided that a tiebreaker race would be held in California in one week. So, McQueen climbed into his trailer and set off with his driver, Mack. "California, here we come!"

Later, after many hours of driving, a weary Mack started to pull off the road. "Just stoppin' off for a quick breather, kid. Ole Mack needs a rest."

But McQueen wanted to be the first one to California. "Absolutely not! We're driving straight through all night until we get to California. We agreed to it."

Poor Mack kept driving while McQueen went to sleep in the trailer. Mack tried to stay awake, but he was exhausted. As he started to doze off some road pranksters began tossing him back and forth across the lanes. In the jostling, the trailer door accidentally opened. When one of the pranksters sneezed, Mack was startled awake, causing McQueen to slip off the ramp of the trailer and into the middle of the oncoming traffic!

Jolted awake, McQueen looked everywhere for his driver. "Mack! Mack! Mack, wait for me!" He followed a truck off the Interstate, but it wasn't Mack.

Confused and lost, McQueen zoomed past a sign that read 'Radiator Springs' when a police cruiser turned on its siren.

"Oh, no."

As McQueen slowed down, Sheriff's car backfired. McQueen mistook the sound. "He's shooting at me! Why's he shooting at me?"

Terrified, he zoomed into the little town of Radiator Springs, where he lost control and crashed into just about everything. He even got tangled with the town statue and dragged it down the road. When it was all over, McQueen was dangling upside down, caught in telephone wires, and the road was ruined. Sheriff glared at him. "Boy, you're in a heap of trouble."

The next morning, McQueen awoke to find himself being greeted by a rusty old tow truck. "Morning, Sleepin' Beauty!"

"Ahhhh! Take whatever you want, just don't hurt me!" McQueen tried to race away, but he couldn't move. The town had put a parking boot on his tyre.

The tow truck smiled. "You're funny, I like you already! My name's Mater."

"Mater?"

"Yeah, like Tuh-mater but without the 'tuh'."

Just then Sheriff rolled up. "What did I tell you about talking to the accused?"

"To not to."

"Well, quit your yappin' and tow this delinquent road hazard to Traffic Court."

The next thing McQueen knew, he was in a courtroom filled with angry townsfolk.

Sheriff spoke, "Anyone want to be his lawyer?"

Mater volunteered, "I'll do it, Sheriff!"

Just then the doors burst open. "All rise, the honourable Doc Hudson presiding!"

An official looking car named Doc rolled onto a lift and was raised to the top of the judge's podium. "Alright, I wanna know who's responsible for wrecking my town, Sheriff. I want his hood on a platter."

But for some strange reason, after Doc took one look at McQueen, he stopped short. "Throw him outta here, Sheriff. Case dismissed!"

McQueen couldn't believe his good luck.

Then a beautiful Porsche entered. "Sorry I'm late, Your Honour."

Thinking she was from his lawyer's office, McQueen interrupted, "Hey, thanks for coming, but we're all set. He's letting me go."

But Sally wasn't from McQueen's lawyer's office – she was the town attorney. McQueen was stunned when she begged Doc to reconsider. "Come on, make this guy fix the road. The town needs this."

Sally told the court that if it wasn't fixed the town wouldn't survive, and since McQueen was the one that did the damage, he should be the one responsible for fixing it.

"So, what do you want him to do?"

"FIX THE ROAD!"

Reluctantly, Doc changed his mind. So, McQueen was sentenced to remain in Radiator Springs and fix the road.

Later that day, Doc introduced McQueen to Bessie, a road-paving machine. "So we're gonna hitch you up to sweet Bessie, and you're gonna pull her nice."

"Whoa, whoa, whoa! How long is this gonna take?"

"Well, if a fella does it right, should take him about five days."

When McQueen heard this he knew he'd never make his race. As soon as Mater removed his parking boot he zoomed away, leaving them in a cloud of dust. "Woo-hoo! Goodbye, Radiator Springs!"

But just then McQueen's engine began to sputter. "No, no, no, no. Outta gas? How can I be out of gas?"

Sheriff and Sally caught up with him. "Boy, we ain't as dumb as you think we are."

"How did you – ?"

"We siphoned your gas while you were passed out. Ka-chow!"

It didn't take McQueen long to realize that the sooner he finished repairing the road the sooner he was going to make it to California. So, he quickly set to work and within an hour had finished the job. "Just say thank you and I'll be on my way."

But as the townsfolk looked at the road all they saw was a bumpy mess of splattered tar. "It looks awful."

"Look, Doc said when I finished, I could go. That was the deal."

Doc pulled up. "The deal was you fix the road, not make it worse. Now scrape it off!"

"Hey, look, grandpa, I'm not a bulldozer, I'm a race car."

"Whoa – is that right? Then why don't we just have a little race, me and you. If you win, you go and I fix the road. If I win, you do the road MY way."

McQueen happily accepted Doc's challenge. He felt there was no way he could lose.

Later, at a dirt track outside of town, the two cars sat at the starting line. The whole town was watching.

Luigi, the tyre store owner, was the starter. "On your mark, get set … GO!"

McQueen took off like a bullet, leaving Doc sitting in his dust. After a few moments Doc slowly started down the track. It looked like there was no way he would ever catch McQueen. But just then, McQueen, who was heading into a turn, lost control and fell off a cliff, landing in a cactus patch.

Doc caught up to him. "You drive like you fix roads … lousy."

After losing to Doc, McQueen went back to repairing the road. He worked all through the night but this time he did the work properly.

When the townsfolk woke the next morning they discovered a beautiful new patch of road. "E' bellisima! It is like it was paved by angels!"

As everyone enjoyed taking a spin on the new road, McQueen asked Sheriff to escort him to the dirt track. He wanted to get the turn he missed the day before. He tried again and again, but he kept skidding out.

Then McQueen realized Doc was watching. Doc tried to coach him, "If you're going hard enough left, you'll find yourself turning right."

But McQueen dismissed Doc's advice. What did he know about racing? "Crazy grandpa car."

The next morning McQueen was back at work on the road. All of the townsfolk were so inspired by how wonderful it looked that they began sprucing up their shops. The whole town was starting to look brand new. Sally stopped by and said McQueen could leave the impound and stay at the Cozy Cone Motel she owned.

That night Mater was in charge of watching McQueen. He took him out tractor tipping – a strange game where you sneak up on sleeping tractors and scare them with a loud noise. When the tractors woke up they were so startled that they would tip over. After sharing some laughs, they headed back to town.

As they drove, Mater teased McQueen. "You're in love with Miss Sally." As Mater continued teasing, he drove backwards. McQueen had never seen anything like it.

"Will you stop that? It's creeping me out – you're going to wreck or something."

"Wreck? Shoot, I'm the world's best backwards driver." Then Mater put on an amazing display of backwards driving.

"Whoa! That was incredible! How'd you do that?"

"I'll teach you if you want."

"Maybe I'll use it in my big race."

"What's so important about this race of yours anyway?"

"I've been dreaming about it my whole life. I'll be the first rookie in history ever to win it and when I do, we're talking a big new sponsor with private helicopters – "

"Hey you think maybe one day I could get a ride in one of them helicopters?"

"Yeah, yeah, yeah, sure, sure."

Mater couldn't have been happier. "I knew it! I knowed I made a good choice."

"In what?"

"My best friend. See you tomorrow, buddy!"

The next day, as McQueen waited for Sheriff to give him his ration of gas, he peeked into Doc's garage. It was a mess. "Whoa, Doc – time to clean out the garage, buddy, come on."

It was then that McQueen stumbled upon something unbelievable.

Just then, Doc entered. "The sign says 'Stay Out'."

"You have three Piston Cups. You're the 'Hudson Hornet'!" Doc slammed the door in McQueen's face, but McQueen was so excited he raced to Flo's cafe to tell everyone. But when he told them the news, no one believed him.

Then Sally invited McQueen to go for a drive. As they playfully raced up the mountain, McQueen was awed by the beautiful surroundings. When they got to the top, McQueen turned to Sally. "How does a Porsche wind up in a place like this?"

"Well, it's really pretty simple. I was an attorney in L.A., living life in the fast lane – "

"Oh, you were, were you?"

"And you know what? It never felt … happy."

"Yeah … I mean, really?"

"Yeah, so I left California – just drove and drove and finally broke down right here. Doc fixed me up. Flo took me in. Well, they all did. And I never left."

McQueen began to understand how much the

town and its inhabitants meant to her. Finally, Sally shared
her dream of returning Radiator Springs to its glory days.
When they got back to town McQueen thanked her. "Thanks
for the drive. I had a great time. It's kind of nice to slow down
every once in a while."

A little while later, McQueen came upon Doc racing alone out at the dirt track. He was truly impressed. When Doc realized he was being watched he left, but McQueen followed him back to his garage. "Doc, hold it, seriously, your driving's incredible!"

"Wonderful. Now go away."

"Hey, I mean it, you've still got it! Under the hood you and I are the same."

"WE ARE NOT THE SAME, UNDERSTAND? NOW GET OUT."

Doc went on to tell McQueen how the racing world had betrayed him long ago after he had a big crash.

"Doc, I'm not them."

"Oh, yeah? When is the last time you cared about

something except yourself, hot rod? Just finish that road and get outta here!"

Early the next morning, the townsfolk awoke to find the road finished and no sign of McQueen. Flo expressed what they were all thinking, "He's gone?"

Just then McQueen appeared. Everyone was elated. "I knowed you wouldn't leave without saying goodbye."

"What are you doing here, son? You're gonna miss your race."

"Well you know I can't go just yet."

Then McQueen said he needed new tyres from Luigi and Guido – which made them overjoyed. "Our first real customer in years!"

Next, McQueen got a case of Fillmore's organic fuel, some night vision goggles from Sarge, bumper stickers from Lizzie and a new paint job from Ramone. When his makeover was complete Sally couldn't believe her eyes. She knew what McQueen was doing. "Oh my goodness, it looks like you've helped everybody in town."

McQueen even had a surprise for Sally. On his cue, the townsfolk turned on their newly repaired neon signs. Sally was amazed. The town was just like in its heyday.

That night, the townsfolk cheerfully cruised under the new neon glow.

Suddenly, a hoard of vehicles swarmed into town. A helicopter hovered overhead. "We have found McQueen!" In an instant, the town was filled with reporters shouting and pushing. "McQueen! Will you still race for the Piston Cup?"

In the chaos, Mack pulled up and urged McQueen that it was time to go. He tried to say goodbye to Sally, but no words would come.

She spoke for him. "Thank you. Thanks for everything."

"It was just a road."

"No – it was much more than that. Good luck in California. I hope you find what you're looking for." Then she backed into the crowd and disappeared.

"Sally! Sally!"

As Mack pulled McQueen's trailer out of town, the swarm of reporters followed.

After things quieted down, Sally was shocked to learn that Doc had called the reporters to tell them where McQueen was. "It's best for everyone, Sally."

"Best for everyone, or best for you?"

A few days later, McQueen should have been focused, but as he stood at the starting line of the big race all he could think of was Sally. He snapped out of his daydream to find the race had started without him.

As he tried to catch up to The King and Chick, McQueen started daydreaming again about Radiator Springs and his drive with Sally. When he snapped out of it he was heading straight for the wall! He hit his brakes hard and spun into the infield. McQueen was about to give up when a familiar voice came over his radio, "Hey, kid – you alright?"

"I don't know, Mack. I … I … I don't – "

"I didn't come all this way to see you quit."

It was Doc! And when McQueen looked toward Pit Row he saw all of his friends from Radiator Springs. "Guys! You're here! I can't believe this!"

That's when Doc took over as his new crew chief. "Kid, get back out there."

Energized by his friends, McQueen pushed hard and was soon back into the race. He was over a whole lap behind. The track announcer called the action, "McQueen passes them on the inside!"

"You're goin' great, kid, just keep your head on."

On the next lap as McQueen tried to squeeze past, Chick bumped him, spinning him around backwards. But instead of falling behind, McQueen used Mater's backward driving technique and zoomed past him! Mater beamed. "I taught him that! Ka-chow!"

"What a move by McQueen! He's caught up to the leaders!"

Chick was not about to come in behind McQueen. As he tried to overtake the rookie he bumped into him, causing one of his tyres to blow. "Doc, I'm flat, I'm flat!" McQueen pulled into the pits where his friend Guido performed the fastest pit stop ever.

With new tyres on, McQueen roared back onto the track. After a few more laps, the white flag waved. It was the final lap. Doc encouraged him, "This is it, kiddo. You got four turns left."

The three cars screamed down the track. As McQueen tried to pass them on the inside, Chick bumped his rear end and sent him spinning towards the infield. But McQueen had one last trick up his sleeve. Using Doc's 'turn right to go left' move, McQueen shot himself back onto the track and into the lead!

But as McQueen headed toward the chequered flag, he heard the crowd gasp. Chick had rammed into The King, knocking him out of the race. Up on the stadium screen, McQueen saw The King battered in the infield. It reminded him of Doc's big crash. Suddenly, instead of crossing the finish line, McQueen slammed on his brakes and went back to help the former champion.

The King was confused.

"What are
you doing, kid?"
"I think The King should finish
his last race." Then, in an amazing display
of good sportsmanship, McQueen pushed The King
across the finish line. The crowd went wild, knowing that
they were witnessing something very special. Because even
though McQueen had finished in last place, he had shown
everyone what a real champion is made of.

A few days later, Sally stopped at the top of the mountain admiring the view of Radiator Springs, when McQueen surprised her. "I hear this place is back on the map."

"It is?"

"Yeah, there's some rumour floating around that some hot shot Piston Cup race car is setting up his big racing headquarters here."

"Really? Oh, well, there goes the town." And with that, Sally raced off.

After a second, McQueen happily took off after her. "Yeah! Ka-chow!"